T0380435

THE
HOUSE
RELATIONSHIPS
BUILT

Other works by Angela Pedigo:

Covered By His Grace

12 Steps of Armor

THE
HOUSE
RELATIONSHIPS
BUILT

Reconstructing Relationships
from the Ground Up!

Angela Pedigo

WESTBOW
PRESS®
A DIVISION OF THOMAS NELSON
& ZONDERVAN

WestBow Press books may be ordered through booksellers or by contacting:

WestBow Press
A Division of Thomas Nelson & Zondervan
1663 Liberty Drive
Bloomington, IN 47403
www.westbowpress.com
844-714-3454

All Scriptures are taken from the NEW AMERICAN STANDARD BIBLE®, Copyright © 1960, 1962, 1963, 1968, 1971, 1972, 1973, 1975, 1977, 1995 by The Lockman Foundation. Used by permission.

Google's English Dictionary Powered by Oxford Languages, Copyright 2023, Oxford University Press, All rights reserved. URL: languages.oup.com

ISBN: 979-8-3850-3227-3 (sc)
ISBN: 979-8-3850-3228-0 (hc)
ISBN: 979-8-3850-3229-7 (e)

Library of Congress Control Number: 2024917734

Print information available on the last page.

WestBow Press rev. date: 10/1/2024

THE
HOUSE
RELATIONSHIPS
BUILT

Reconstructing Relationships
from the Ground Up!

Angela Pedigo

WESTBOW
PRESS®
A DIVISION OF THOMAS NELSON
& ZONDERVAN

WestBow Press books may be ordered through booksellers or by contacting:

WestBow Press
A Division of Thomas Nelson & Zondervan
1663 Liberty Drive
Bloomington, IN 47403
www.westbowpress.com
844-714-3454

Because of the dynamic nature of the Internet, any web addresses or links contained in this book may have changed since publication and may no longer be valid. The views expressed in this work are solely those of the author and do not necessarily reflect the views of the publisher, and the publisher hereby disclaims any responsibility for them.

Any people depicted in stock imagery provided by Getty Images are models, and such images are being used for illustrative purposes only. Certain stock imagery © Getty Images.

All Scriptures are taken from the NEW AMERICAN STANDARD BIBLE®, Copyright © 1960, 1962, 1963, 1968, 1971, 1972, 1973, 1975, 1977, 1995 by The Lockman Foundation. Used by permission.

Google's English Dictionary Powered by Oxford Languages, Copyright 2023, Oxford University Press, All rights reserved. URL: languages.oup.com

ISBN: 979-8-3850-3227-3 (sc)
ISBN: 979-8-3850-3228-0 (hc)
ISBN: 979-8-3850-3229-7 (e)

Library of Congress Control Number: 2024917734

Print information available on the last page.

WestBow Press rev. date: 10/1/2024

Let's Get to Work!

Healthy relationships do not just happen by luck or chance. They take work which usually begins with correcting your definition of love. Your current understanding may be based on codependent patterns forming from hurtful experiences in the past, and those codependent patterns hinder healthy relationships.

The House Relationships Built provides a blueprint of how to reconstruct relationships the way Jesus intended us to love one another in the first and second greatest commandment of all found in Matthew 22:37–40 (NASB),

> And He said to him, "You shall love the Lord your God with all your heart and with all your soul, and with all your mind. This is the great and foremost commandment. The second is like it, You shall love your neighbor as yourself. On these two commandments depends the whole Law and the Prophets."

This book has been written based on my own personal journey of breaking the hold codependence had in my life. I am a certified professional life and recovery coach, not a therapist or counselor. I share insights on how codependent patterns affected me and how the Holy Spirit led me to deconstruct my beliefs about relationships while teaching me about the love Jesus has for me. Through my connection with Jesus, I learned to properly love myself and others.

The material in this book is not a replacement for therapy or counseling of any kind. It is meant to be utilized as a way of connecting or reconnecting your spiritual life with God and living more Christlike through biblical principles.

Studying this book with someone you trust is also beneficial. The Bible teaches that,

> As Iron sharpens iron, so one person sharpens another. (Proverbs 27:17 NASB)

I encourage married couples to seek help from a counselor or therapist to navigate any marital issues.

Let's venture down this road together and let real love, God's love, grow your heart and mind today. Let the building begin!

Angela Pedigo

Contents

The Blueprint: Steps for Healthy Relationships

1. We admit that we may not really know who we are and that our lives have been affected by the lack of having a healthy relationship with ourselves.

   But now, LORD, You are our Father; We are the clay, and You our potter, And all of us are the work of Your hand. (Isaiah 64:8 NASB)

2. We believe God can teach us who He made us to be.

   For You created my innermost parts; You wove me in my mother's womb. (Psalm 139:13 NASB)

3. We became willing to form a relationship with God as we begin to understand Him.

   Behold, I stand at the door and knock; if anyone hears My voice and opens the door, I will come in to him and will dine with him, and he with Me. (Revelation 3:20 NASB)

4. We made a searching and fearless moral inventory of ourselves to understand how the words and actions of ourselves and others have shaped our lives.

    Search me, God, and know my heart; Put me to the test and know my anxious thoughts; And see if there is any hurtful way in me, And lead me in the everlasting way. (Psalm 139:23–24 NASB)

5. We admitted to ourselves, to God, and to another human being the exact nature of our wrongs.

    One who conceals his wrongdoings will not prosper, But one who confesses and abandons them will find compassion. (Proverbs 28:13 NASB)

6. We became entirely ready to have God remove any fear of abandonment, along with the belief that we are not enough for ourselves, for God, or for others.

    The LORD is for me; I will not fear; What can man do to me? (Psalm 118:6 NASB)

7. We humbly asked Him to remove anything that hinders us from being our true self in His image.

    Therefore be imitators of God, as beloved children; and walk in love, just as Christ also loved you and gave Himself up for us, an offering and a sacrifice to God as a fragrant aroma. (Ephesians 5:1–2 NASB)

8. We made a list of all the persons we had harmed and became willing to make amends to them all.

But now you also, rid yourselves of all of them: anger, wrath, malice, slander, and obscene speech from your mouth. Do not lie to one another, since you stripped off the old self with its evil practices, and have put on the new self, which is being renewed to a true knowledge according to the image of the One who created it. (Colossians 3:8–10 NASB)

9. We made direct amends to such people whenever possible, except when doing so would injure them or others.

So, as those who have been chosen of God, holy and beloved, put on a heart of compassion, kindness, humility, gentleness, and patience; bearing with one another, and forgiving each other, whoever has a complaint against anyone; just as the Lord forgave you, so must you do also. (Colossians 3:12–13 NASB)

10. We continue taking personal inventory, and when we are wrong, we promptly admit it, so that we keep our relationship with God, self, and others free and at peace.

If possible, so far as it depends on you, be at peace with all people. (Romans 12:18 NASB)

11. We continue to improve our relationship with God by staying in daily contact with Him through meditation, praise, and prayer; seeking His will for us and the courage to carry it out.

   In all your ways acknowledge Him, And He will make your paths straight. (Proverbs 3:6 NASB)

12. Having gained a relationship with God and ourselves, we strive to form healthy relationships with others, allowing God to lead, guide, and direct us in all our affairs.

   Above all, keep fervent in your love for one another, because love covers a multitude of sins. (1 Peter 4:8 NASB)

> Be strong and courageous, do not
> be afraid or in dread of them, for the
> LORD your God is the One who is going
> with you. He will not desert you or
> abandon you.
>
> —Deuteronomy 31:6 (NASB)

What Is Love?

What is love? Many people are searching for the answer to this loaded question in the wrong places. Love is an action word, not just a feeling or emotion. Feelings come and go, and emotions can lead us wrong. The Bible warns about chasing after emotions.

> The heart is more deceitful than all else and is desperately sick; who can understand it? (Jeremiah 17:9 NASB)

For a relationship to last, love must last. So how do you prevent love from fleeting? You first need to understand its characteristics. Let's look at 1 Corinthians 13 to explore the biblical definition of love in any type of relationship. Verses 1–3 indicate that no matter what abilities you have or what good works you do, if you do not have love in your heart, it is of no benefit.

> If I speak with the tongues of mankind and of angels, but do not have love, I have become a noisy gong or a clanging cymbal. If I have the

gift of prophesy and know all mysteries and all knowledge, and if I have all faith so as to remove mountains, but do not have love, I am nothing. And if I give away all my possessions to charity, and if I surrender my body so that I may glory, but do not have love, it does me no good. (1 Corinthians 13:1–3 NASB)

The question then becomes *how* do you use your abilities and *why* do you do the things you do for someone. Is it out of personal gain, manipulation, or purely out of love? These scriptures call you to search yourselves by examining your motives.

Do you find yourself going back to former toxic relationships because you truly love this person or so that you aren't alone? If the decision to return to a toxic relationship is based on the fear that no one else may ever want you, then it wasn't necessarily love that took you back. It may have been fear of those what-ifs and unknowns about your future.

Let's look at what the rest of this chapter has to say about love. Verse 4 states "Love is patient, love is kind …" To know if love exists, you must take an honest look at both yourself and the other person. Do you have patience with one another? Do you show kindness to one another in words and actions?

This same verse begins describing what love is and then takes a turn. It clearly portrays characteristics of what love is not.

It is not jealous; love does not brag, it is not arrogant. It does not act disgracefully, it does not seek its own benefit; it is not provoked, does not keep an account of a wrong suffered, it does not rejoice in unrighteousness, but rejoices with the truth; it keeps every confidence, it believes all things, hopes all things, endures all things. (1 Corinthians 13:4–7 NASB)

The chart below breaks down these scriptures to create a visual of the qualities of any relationship.

Love is	Love is not
Patient	Jealous
Kind	Bragging
Truthful	Arrogant
Trustworthy	Acting disgracefully
Believes in you	Selfish
Hopeful for you	Provoking to anger or sin
Enduring all things with you	Unforgiving/unforgetting
	Excited about wrongdoing

If love appears to be lacking, there is hope. With a few areas of work, it *could* turn your relationship into an amazing connection! Relationships based on love should want what is best for you, encourage you, and support you. Neither person in the relationship should tear one another down. This includes the relationship you have with yourself.

Here are some questions to think about:

1. Before reading this chapter, what was your idea of love? Was it the same or different?

2. Choose a connection you tend to find difficult and circle all of the characteristics in both columns on the chart above that apply to this relationship.

3. Now, look at the chart as it pertains to your own actions. Place a checkmark by the actions that describe your role in that same relationship. Do you believe your actions are based on love? Why or why not?

4. How do you treat yourself, such as do you speak kindly about yourself? Do you encourage and believe in yourself? Or do you think more negatively toward yourself? Explain.

5. Now go back over the chart and list below all of the actions that are present in your relationship with yourself. Would you say your relationship with yourself is based on love? Why or why not?

6. Do you fear personal growth? Why or why not?

7. Think about the thoughts you often have toward yourself. Would you say these same things to others? Why or why not?

CHAPTER 1

Step 1

We admit that we may not really know who we are and that our lives have been affected by the lack of having a healthy relationship with ourselves.

> But now, LORD, You are our Father;
> We are the clay, and You our potter,
> And all of us are the work of Your hand.
> —Isaiah 64:8 (NASB)

> For through the grace given to me I say to everyone among you not to think more highly of himself than he ought to think; but to think so as to have sound judgment, as God has allotted to each a measure of faith.
>
> —Romans 12:3 (NASB)

Relate to Form a Relationship

Relationships can be one of the hardest connections to understand. To build a healthy relationship, it's important to build it from the ground up. To begin, let's look at the root word of *relationship*, which is the word *relate*. The definition of *relate*, according to *Oxford Dictionaries*, is "to make or show connection between; feel sympathy with; identify with." We will examine three relationships: how you relate to yourself, to God, and finally to others through connection and identity.

When you don't learn about yourself, isolation can create feelings of loneliness and abandonment. You can also block God and others out of your life to create intentional isolation if you have trust issues. This state of being makes it difficult to find joy and fulfillment.

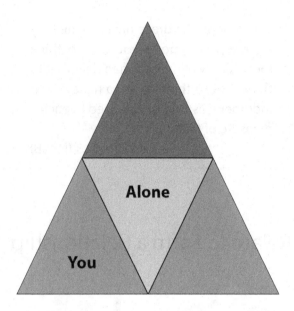

Once you learn more about who you are, the next step is to learn what God says about you, how He feels about you, and what plans He has for you. It is one thing to know who God is and believe in Him. Healing comes from building a *relationship* with Him.

Wholeness is when you know who you are, you have a meaningful relationship with God, and you understand how to form healthy relationships with others. Understanding how to trust, how to establish boundaries when necessary, and how to include God's direction and guidance for your life are instrumental in successful relationships.

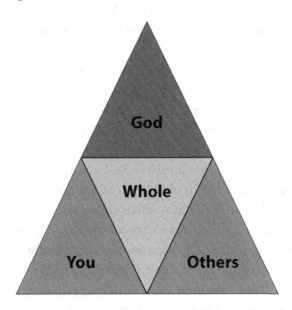

Sometimes people want to rush into relationships carrying hurt from the past with them. These hurts run the risk of creating unhealthy codependent patterns. It's like building a house; you cannot place the roof on without first digging the footers, pouring the concrete, laying the foundation, and then framing the house. When a relationship begins with others in mind first, it's like trying to build the house backward. The relationship *has a hole* rather than *being whole*.

Codependency is defined by *Oxford Languages* as *excessive emotional or psychological reliance on a partner.* This reliance can come from an emotional or physical abandonment and/or feelings of not being good enough for others. Some examples of codependent roles are controllers, people pleasers, saviors or rescuers, and victims, to name a few. I have personally found myself in each of these different roles in the past. The role I played depended on the role the other person in the relationship was playing. For example, if I saw them as a victim but they didn't see themselves that way, I became a rescuer by trying to make their life better and doing all I could for them in hopes that they would find me valuable and wouldn't leave.

If I felt the person was trying to rescue me, I would become angry and push them away, becoming the controller, to keep them from getting too close or smothering me. The fact that someone perceived me as a victim angered me because of my pride. I didn't think I was weak, and I didn't want to be seen that way. I saw myself as an independent survivor. So I controlled the situation and became quite harsh, trying to get the person to give up and walk away. Reacting this way often drove the other person to start speaking and acting as a victim of their own circumstances apart from me, trying to get me to save them. If they could get me to feel sorry for them, then maybe I wouldn't walk away. That would anger me even more. I didn't want to take care of anybody. I wanted to be taken care of, or so I thought. But when someone would take care of me, I pushed them away as well, feeling like I would owe them something, which could trap me in a relationship I didn't want.

In another relationship, I was so controlled by that person that I felt isolated from my family and friends who loved me. This person sometimes isolated me on purpose, knowing that if I was around those who loved me, they could see what was going on better than I could. They might just talk me into leaving the person. This controller role beat me down so low that I was convinced I couldn't ever escape. I just kept taking the abuse. They would pick a fight to have a reason to leave. When they were ready to come back, they would return only to blame me for the fight, convincing me it was my fault when I had done nothing wrong. I would go as far as believing it and agreeing with them, taking the blame and finding myself apologizing for something they did. Why? Fear of abandonment. This cycle was the most abusive to me personally, and it took an intervention of the Holy Spirit to help me escape it.

Anytime I found myself in the controller role, I only wanted to control the situation for self-preservation. I believed if I wasn't in control, I could get blindsided or miss something like a red flag that would help me know when to abort the mission. I wanted to be loved, but I didn't want to be hurt anymore. Trusting others was hard at that point because I wouldn't take time to heal. I wouldn't take time to know who I was, let alone love myself for me, whether anyone was there or not. If I had loved myself enough, I wouldn't have had a need to set what I thought were strong boundaries around us as a couple to protect us. I had no concept of what boundaries actually looked like. I would try to box our relationship in by creating parameters we would operate as a couple to keep us both safe. But that never worked either. It was completely out of fear, not a desire to dominate. I hated feeling a need to control something. I just wanted to feel safe and free and didn't know how to get to that point.

The cycles kept repeating and creating more hurt with each relationship. But I want you to know there is hope! And it started with learning who I was as an individual, not attaching my identity to others' opinions of me.

When a relationship starts, the excitement is like the honeymoon stage, with each person filling the holes from the past in the other's heart. It seems great at first until it loses the ability to fill those holes because new holes start to form.

People entertain these types of relationships for different reasons. Some do so because they don't know anything different. It may be all they have ever seen or experienced. Some do so to avoid being alone. One time, a lady told me that she would rather have bad love than no love at all. That was before she went through her own healing journey. Loneliness is cold and deafening when left alone with thoughts of the past. The hurts and regrets bouncing around inside our minds are not the best company. So we fill space and time with anyone who can keep us out of that alone state.

For me, having someone around, no matter if it was a healthy or unhealthy situation, helped keep those thoughts shoved down deep by keeping me in the present moment.

There are other times when someone might be addicted to chaos, therefore surrounding themselves with chaotic situations. Times of peace are almost disturbing because living in peace can be so uncomfortable for someone who has never experienced peace in their lives. I asked a girl once, "When is the last time you recall feeling peace?" She had no answer to the question, and it upset her so much that she walked out of the room. She could not even think about having peace in her life yet. I knew if she could just let Jesus into the areas where she was feeling hurt, He could heal those things and give her peace. But she was not in a place to receive it or even consider it. And that's OK. You can't force anyone to feel something they are not ready for or capable of feeling for whatever reason. As we keep moving forward, this, among many other reasons, is why it is important to form a relationship with Jesus, the Prince of Peace!

Are you shocked at this point? If you are like me, you may be identifying several of your relationships that have fallen into these different scenarios. It is eye-opening, to say the least. Now let me explain how I've found a healthy relationship is supposed to function. I really prayed for wisdom to understand how God made a relationship to be healthy. The first relationship that came to mind was God's relationship with Adam and Eve in the Garden of Eden. Before the fall of man in Genesis 3, Adam and Eve communed with God in innocence and peace. They could just *be*. The connection between God, Adam, and Eve was peaceful, gentle, and trusting. It was easy. Can you imagine a relationship where you feel like you could just be you and still be loved? Dealing with the hurt from the past is essential for this kind of connection.

For those of you who are in marriages that may reflect some of the patterns we've discussed, it's easy to be hyperfocused on your spouse's role due to the hurt you may feel. But as you work this program, your focus is best spent on you and your role in the relationship. Begin praying now for your spouse, asking God to bring them to their own personal journey with Him while you are working on yours. I've found many times in my life that the problem wasn't the other person; it was actually me or how I felt about the situation that needed to change. And when I embraced that, the whole situation changed for the better.

Now, let's take a look at how you relate to *you*. Your perspective of yourself may be healthy or unhealthy depending on the environment you grew up in and/or what you have already worked through. The earliest shaping of your identity comes from the words and actions of others such as parents, family, friends, strangers, and possibly even yourself. These words and actions could be healthy or unhealthy, supported or neglected, etc. When you adopt these ideas as truth about yourself, you risk acting on them. For example, you may have this recurring thought in your mind, "If they say I'm *that*, I must be *that*; therefore, I might as well do what *that* does." People modify their behaviors based on what their beliefs are about themselves.

Whether others have ever poured into you or whether they didn't give you that time and attention, it's now time to pour into yourself. No one is necessarily going to nurture your strengths, abilities, and talents that may have gone unrecognized somewhere along the way. But the only thing that can stop you now from doing so is yourself.

To find the foundation of what you believe about yourself, try answering the following questions:

1. What do you believe about you? List below.

2. Are your beliefs about yourself based on someone else's perspective or your own? Explain.

3. Now go back to the answer to the previous question and note whether these beliefs are fact or fiction.

4. What are you good at?

5. What do you struggle with?

6. How do you want to see yourself? Consider this question with a goal in mind. At the end of your life, what do you

want others to be able to say about you? What testimony do you want to leave behind? Things to consider are your morals, service to others, goals, accomplishments, etc. This is not a question to bring discouragement. It is establishing a destination point to set your sights on as we move forward.

Becoming Self-Aware

> So Jesus was saying to those Jews who had believed Him, "If you continue in My word, then you are truly My disciples; and you will know the truth, and the truth will set you free."
> —John 8:31–32 (NASB)

The definition of self-awareness according to *Oxford Languages* is a "conscious knowledge of one's own character, feelings, motives, and desires." Let's break this definition down for a deeper understanding of what is needed to be self-aware.

1. Character–What distinctly makes you who you are.

2. Feelings–Feelings are secondary to emotions. Our feelings are what we feel based on the emotion driving it. Emotions are deeper than feelings, and sometimes, we may not understand the emotions we experience.

3. Motives—Motives are *why* you choose to do the things you do. They are not what you convince yourself or others is your "why." Motives are the real root reason, often based on some hidden emotion.

4. Desires—Your desires are what you long for.

One thing I found in coaching others is that oftentimes, the last component of self-awareness that people allow to drive their actions is character. Character is a choice. Everything else is emotion driven. If you decide who you want to be, and if you intend to be that person no matter what, then you will have times in your life when you will have to refuse your feelings and desires to actually *be* the person you want to be. When character drives your desires, feelings, and motives, you are choosing who you want to be. Jesus puts this in perspective:

> Then Jesus said to His disciples, "If anyone wants to come after Me, he must deny himself, take up his cross, and follow Me." (Matthew 16:24 NASB)

Accept that you cannot change the past or where you've been. Accept where you are at today. Claim where you are going in the future! Start by answering these questions below:

1. What order do you find yourself acting on the four components of self-awareness discussed in this section? For example, do your feelings tend to drive your motives, which lead to your desires, and then reflect in your character? Or is it some other sequence?

2. Meditate on the following scriptures and write down how they speak to you.

    Psalm 139:13–14:

    Proverbs 29:18:

3. Imagine Jesus sitting across from you as you read John 15:1–17. What do you believe Jesus is saying to you verse by verse? Make it personal by journaling how He wants you to apply each verse to your life today.

CHAPTER 2

Step 2

We believe God can teach us who He made us to be.

> For you created my innermost parts;
> You wove me in my mother's womb.
> —Psalm 139:13 (NASB)

> And this is eternal life, that they may know You, the only true God, and Jesus Christ whom You have sent.
>
> —John 17:3 (NASB)

How Do You Relate to God?

In order to have a relationship with God, you must get to know Him. If you don't really know Him, you won't know where to put Him in your life. Knowing God is very different from knowing *about* God or just believing in Him.

If God is currently not a part of your life, you certainly won't lose anything by learning who He is. Then you get to decide if you want to form a relationship with Him. As you think about that decision, understand that *true* healing comes from a relationship with God.

To Relate or not to Relate …
Is That Your Question?

Acts 17:24–28 reflect that God is supreme or sovereign. He is our provider. He lives in heaven and is the Creator of all. He is the Father of Jesus Christ. These are just some of the characteristics of His being.

Let's look at how God feels about you. Read the following scriptures to get to know Him better and what His Word says about you.

    1.   He thinks about you—thoughts of peace and not evil; … to give you a hope and a future (Jeremiah 29:11 NASB).

2. He cares for His creations (birds, flowers, etc.), yet He cares for you even more. He knows everything about you (Matthew 10:29–31 NASB).

3. He will not throw you away or abandon you (Psalm 94:14 NASB).

4. He gives you strength and courage, not fear, worry, depression, etc. He is with you wherever you go (Joshua 1:9 NASB).

5. Nothing can separate you from His love for you (Romans 8:38–39 NASB).

6. You were created by Him to do good things (Ephesians 2:10 NASB).

7. He gave you certain gifts or abilities when He created you (Romans 12:3–8 NASB). These gifts are listed below from the scriptures:

   • Prophesy—the ability to hear from God
   • Ministry—serving others
   • Exhortation—influencing others
   • Teaching—sharing knowledge and wisdom with others
   • Giver—giving to others liberally or freely
   • Leader—one who leads diligently or carefully
   • Mercy—cheerfully forgives with ease

There is one common thread among these gifts. They are all gifts that pertain to relating to God and others, which further validates why we need to know how to have healthy relationships.

You can use these gifts in many ways. For example, you can teach someone good things or bad things. You can lead someone in good ways or bad ways. You can exhort or influence someone to do good or to do harm to themselves or others. These gifts are given to you, but it is up to you as to how you are going to use them, whether for worldly gain or for God's kingdom. Here in lies free will. God doesn't force Himself on you nor does He force you to use the gifts He gave you for His kingdom. You have to choose Him if you want a relationship with Him. Below are some questions for you to consider about God and the gifts He gave you.

1. What do you believe about God currently? List below.

2. Which of His gifts do you believe He gave to you? Do you use them for worldly good or heavenly good? Explain.

What Do You Know about Jesus?

> And they all said, "So You are the Son of God?" And He said to them, "You say correctly that I am."
> —Luke 22:70 (NASB)

It is important to know who Jesus is when building a relationship with God. Jesus is the Son of God and Savior of the world.

> For God so loved the world that He gave His only Son, so that everyone who believes in Him will not perish, but have eternal life. For God did not send the Son into the world to judge the world, but so that the world might be saved through Him. The one who believes in Him is not judged; the one who does not believe has been judged already, because he has not believed in the name of the only Son of God. (John 3:16–18 NASB)

Jesus came and died for the sins of all mankind. God's requirement for giving His Son for us in order to be saved from the end times wrath to come is that people must believe in who Jesus is, what He did on the cross, and that God raised Him from the dead three days later. And this belief is not just with the mind. We must believe it with the heart as evidenced in scripture.

> That if you confess with your mouth Jesus as Lord, and believe in your heart that God raised Him from the dead, you will be saved; for with the

21

> heart a person believes, resulting in righteousness, and with the mouth he confesses, resulting in salvation. (Romans 10:9–10 NASB)

After Jesus died on the cross, God raised Him from the dead three days later. Jesus then appeared to his disciples and followers at various times for the next forty days. After those forty days, Jesus ascended to heaven. He did so to prove to His followers that He was alive and that the prophecy in the Old Testament had been fulfilled. He also instructed them to go tell everyone throughout the world the good news, that there is redemption (forgiveness) for their sins once and for all. If they believe in Him with their heart, they can receive this free gift of mercy and grace. And this gift is for everyone!

Jesus also told His disciples that they didn't have to go alone to spread the gospel. When Jesus went to heaven, He left the Holy Spirit here on earth to be a comforter and guide, among many other things. We will discuss more on this in the next chapter.

Now, let's explore Jesus's example of how to relate to God. God is His Father. To get a concept of this relationship, try examining your relationship with your own father. Oftentimes, a person's relationship with their earthly father mirrors how they see God as their heavenly Father before they get to know God. For example, if your earthly father was absent in your life, do you feel like God is a million miles away or nonexistent? If your earthly father was a dictator type, do you envision God sitting on a big throne with a lightning bolt waiting to strike you each time you make a mistake? If you felt like your earthly father didn't care about you as a child, do you have a hard time believing God cares about you?

Some of the ways Jesus built His relationship with His heavenly Father can be found in the following scriptures:

- Matthew 14:23–He would get alone with Him to pray (or communicate).

- Mark 1:35–He would get up early and start His day with Him in prayer.

- Luke 5:16–Jesus's "prayer closet" may have actually been the wilderness.

- Luke 6:12–13–Sometimes He would pray for hours with God (communicating), especially when big decisions were about to be made.

- Luke 22:39–46–Jesus fled to the place he often went to pray when He knew tough times were upon Him, praying for His own strength and focus. He made his requests known to His Father, but would ask for His Father's will to be done over His own. That showed respect.

Jesus taught us in these verses and many more how we can build a father-child relationship with God too.

In Acts 1:9, when Jesus ascended to heaven to be with God right before their very eyes, He left gifts for people as well. The gifts of Jesus are listed in Ephesians 4:11–12. There are five of them, and they are callings on the lives of believers to go and make disciples of all nations. These gifts are apostles, prophets, evangelists, pastors (or preachers), and teachers.

You can learn who Jesus is in character and truth from reading Matthew, Mark, Luke, and John in the Bible. You can see how He handled similar situations you face today, how He conducted Himself in tough times, how He healed people, forgave people, and how He handled things that seemed unbearable. You can also learn His main message: Repent. Repenting means to turn from what road you are on that separates you from Him but rather turn toward God. The message was simple, yet people have made it more complicated through time.

Below is a list of situations you can learn from Jesus and His examples:

- How to handle temptation,
- How to treat others,
- How to give,
- How to pray,
- How to cure anxiety,
- How to not be judgmental,
- How to spot hypocrisy and religious traditions,
- How to love, heal, and forgive,
- How to have compassion,
- How to be obedient,
- How to be loyal,
- How to walk with integrity and honesty, and how to stay the course when things are tough,
- How to deal with false accusations from others about yourself,
- How not to fear what others can do to you,
- How to follow God no matter what others may think,
- How to get rid of evil,
- How to be a friend,
- How to treat children,
- How to serve others as the greatest form of leadership,
- How to be angry and yet not sin,
- How to work hard,
- How to be humble and meek and yet stronger than ever, and
- How to love people anyway.

Jesus can teach you so much about how to carry yourself, how to grow in your relationship with your heavenly Father, and how to prepare you for healthy connections with others.

Check out the following questions to help identify where your relationship is with Jesus today.

1. What was/is your relationship like with your earthly father? Does it mirror how you feel about God as a heavenly Father? Explain.

2. Why is it important for you personally to slip away alone to pray? If you don't do so currently, how do you think prayer time would improve your relationship with God?

3. If you have not believed in Jesus with your heart, what keeps you from experiencing His salvation? If you have taken that step, describe it.

4. Do you think once someone believes in Jesus for that salvation moment, that's all you have to do in your relationship with Him going forward for it to grow? Why or why not?

5. Do you fear that if you learn more about Jesus, you might have more expectations of you living differently? Explain.

6. Review the list of situations you can learn how to handle from Jesus. Which examples are you most interested in learning at this point in your life? What will you do to explore them?

CHAPTER 3

Step 3
We became willing to form a relationship with God as we begin to understand Him.

> Behold, I stand at the door and knock; if anyone hears My voice and opens the door, I will come in to him and will dine with him, and he with Me.
> —Revelation 3:20 (NASB)

> If you love Me, you will keep My commandments. I will ask the Father, and He will give you another Helper, so that He may be with you forever; the Helper is the Spirit of truth, whom the world cannot receive, because it does not see Him or know Him; but you know Him because He remains with you and will be in you.
>
> —John 14:15–17 (NASB)

The Role of the Holy Spirit

Step 3 in this building process is about surrendering and becoming willing to form a relationship with God. Surrender begins just before salvation. Salvation is the beginning of the relationship with Jesus as your Savior and with God as your Father. You are then adopted into the family of God through salvation. To grow that relationship, as with any other relationship, it takes time and interest to build it. Jesus already loves you. This is the point where you begin to love Him back and learn more about Him. For some people, this love comes easy. For others, it can take time to trust that Jesus loved them enough to give His life for them, even before they knew Him.

When you love someone, you want to know more about them, experience more with them, hang out with them, help them, etc. Your relationship with Jesus should look the same way. It doesn't have an end point. Like any other relationship, it will grow at the pace you seek it. This kind of growth is referred to as becoming Christlike. The more we look for Jesus, the more we will find Him.

> Ask, and it will be given to you; seek, and you will find; knock, and it will be opened to you. For everyone who asks receives, and he who seeks finds, and the one who knocks it will be opened. (Matthew 7:7–8 NASB)

Examine these verses, not relating to material things in this life, but in spiritual understanding. In order to grow, you must be willing to travel the spiritual journey of sanctification. Sanctification is the process of not living this life *for* this life, but rather understanding spiritually how to live *in* this life *for* the next life, or eternity. When salvation comes to us, and we have the spirit of Christ living in us, then we need to know how to walk in it and to live in His presence.

It's like when you purchase a new car. The car always has new buttons to push that do different things. These buttons are there as upgrades and features for comfort and ease while driving and traveling in your car. It also comes with an owner's manual to provide you with instructions on care, maintenance, and features, the speed of the car, and the power of the motor. This manual will tell you what kind of fuel is best for optimal performance. Then you get in your car and you drive for a while. You find comfort in being in your car. It's a place where you pray, cry, relax on a ride trying to destress, sing, shout, and experience life, sometimes in ways you feel you can't do outside of your car.

Meet the Holy Spirit, the one Jesus said would come as your helper and guide, among many other things. The Holy Spirit is a lot like this car. When the Holy Spirit comes into your life, you have a new comforter, a new helper in times of need. To understand this relationship fully, read John chapters 14–16. Jesus explains the role of the Holy Spirit, also known as the spirit of truth.

When Jesus ascended to heaven, He left the Holy Spirit here on Earth to help us. The Holy Spirit provides us spiritual gifts when we have Him living within us. These gifts are listed in 1 Corinthians 12:1–11 and consist of the following: knowledge, wisdom, discernment, faith, healing, miracles, prophesy, speaking in tongues, and interpreting tongues. These are not our new personal superpowers. They belong to the Holy Spirit, who grants them to us like a gift in time of need when we seek them out and believe. And they are granted to help the whole body of believers, not for selfish gain. Let's break them down for a better understanding.

1. Knowledge–knowing and understanding God
2. Wisdom–understanding how to apply that knowledge
3. Discernment–the ability to discern right from wrong, good from bad, and what actions to take and when. Sometimes the action is to *not* act at all
4. Faith–believing with your heart amid uncertainty or unknowns
5. Healing–physically, mentally, emotionally, spiritually, etc.
6. Miracles – doing what we cannot possibly do on our own
7. Prophecy – the ability to hear that still small voice of the Holy Spirit leading, guiding, and proclaiming
8. Speaking in tongues–heavenly language prayers; also, the ability of the apostles on the day of Pentecost to speak in the languages they didn't otherwise know

how to speak so that those there could hear the gospel preached in their own languages to understand and therefore believe

9. Interpreting tongues–prophetic interpretation; the ability to understand or know what is being spoken in an unknown language

Now check out the Holy Spirit's "bells and whistles" compared to the comfort of your new car.

New car	Relationship with God
Owner's manual	Bible
Maintenance records	Prayers, journals, etc.
Strange noise	Unknown language
Fuel type	Prayer, praise, worship
Driving on a beautiful day	Gratitude
Music	Worship songs, videos
Trustworthy	Faith, worry-free
Avoiding a wreck	Miracle
Expensive repairs	Provisions to cover it
Warning lights	Prophecy, discernment
Navigation	Plans, prophecy for your life

How well do you know and trust your car? Do you run to your car to get away, escape, find comfort, or get somewhere you can't get to on your own? In this relationship with God, the Holy Spirit functions the same way. The Holy Spirit also moves with how much you accelerate the pedal on your relationship with Him.

If you haven't believed in Jesus for salvation, now is a good time to start seeking Him out in prayer. If you have experienced salvation but have been stagnant in your spiritual growth, this is the time to form a relationship with the Holy Spirit. Pray that the Holy Spirit baptizes you by His spiritual fire; to fill you with His fruits and gifts and to live within you!

CHAPTER 4

Step 4

We made a searching and fearless moral inventory of ourselves to understand how the words and actions of ourselves and others have shaped our lives.

> Search me, God, and know my heart; Put me to the test and know my anxious thoughts; and see if there is any hurtful way in me, and lead me in the everlasting way.
>
> —Psalm 139:23–24 (NASB)

> And do not be conformed to this world, but be transformed by the renewing of your mind, so that you may prove what the will of God is, that which is good and acceptable and perfect.
>
> —Romans 12:2 (NASB)

Let It Begin ... with Me

It's time to dig deeper to understand how the past has shaped your present. Your experiences, good and bad, all play a part in what you believe in, what you value, and how you react to situations. The first relationship you need to build is the one with yourself. Step 4 is the beginning of what can be a painful introduction to you, and you need God's help to do so. This process is necessary because you can't know where you are going if you don't know where you've been. For example, if you are in Nashville, Tennessee, traveling to New York City, and you are given a map of Michigan to New York, it will do you no good. You won't have the map needed to get to your destination. Step 4 is like creating the map of your life. It reflects where you have been and where you are at, so that you have the right direction for where you want to go.

Let's look at your starting point. An example of the areas in your life that may be impacted today by the things in your past might look something like this:

WHEEL OF IMPACT

As you can see, the areas of a person's life being impacted by past hurts are most likely impacting the lives of others around them. Hurt people often pass on that hurt to other people, which is why trauma is passed down from generation to generation when left unaddressed. And that is why the number of people battling codependence is so extremely high in our country. But healed people help other people to heal, and those who heal break the cycle of generational curses. These hurts can stop repeating in your family lineage when you decide to work through your own past. You can relate to your children and others around you differently. The person who breaks the cycle is called a transition person. A transition person chooses to heal, which can change the family tree for those generations who follow after them.

To see what areas of your life are being impacted, let's look at the following challenges and questions.

1. Draw your wheel of impact. What areas of your life do you feel are being impacted today from hurts in the past?

2. Draw your family tree going as far back generationally as you have knowledge of. Once you have the names, list under each name the traumas or hurts you know they experienced or struggles they dealt with. For example, if they suffered from addiction, mental health disorders, abuse, etc., note it.

3. What did you learn from the assignment above?

4. What patterns can you identify that you want to break?

5. What vision do you currently have of where you want to go? Consider which areas you want to overcome as your destination point. Be specific.

Where Am I?

> For through the grace given to me I say to everyone among you not to think more highly of himself than he ought to think; but to think so as to have sound judgment, as God has allotted to each a measure of faith.
>
> —Romans 12:3 (NASB)

There are two stages of relationships we should examine at this point.

Stage 1: Isolation—This is where you feel alone, whether intentionally or unintentionally. The Bible has some insights on this stage.

> One who separates himself seeks his own desire;
> He quarrels against all sound wisdom. (Proverbs 18:1 NASB)

Some people may take a break from *new* relationships while trying to work through hurts or may spend time with the Holy Spirit like Jesus did. Jesus regularly spent time alone with God in prayer. If you are married or in a committed relationship, it is important to carve out some time with God each day to prayerfully do some soul-searching and to seek His direction and guidance. Jesus always came back to His disciples after spending time alone with God. This, however, is not isolation because the Holy Spirit will be with you during those times if you invite Him along for the journey.

True isolation without seeking God is, however, counterproductive to growth. The Bible tells us:

> And let's consider how to encourage one another
> in love and good deeds, not abandoning our own
> meeting together, as is the habit of some people,
> but encouraging one another; and all the more
> as you see the day drawing near. (Hebrew 10:25)

I hope you will consider support groups, counseling, therapy, etc., for additional healing and support. If you have trauma to work through that seems too difficult to face or you feel stuck in the effects of the trauma, counseling or therapy may be for you in addition to growing your relationship with God.

The Bible teaches that we are all parts of a group and without one another, the group isn't complete.

> For the body is not one part, but many. If the foot says, "Because I am not a hand, I am not a part of the body," it is not for this reason any less a part of the body. (1 Corinthians 12:14–15 NASB)

We, as God's children, make up parts of one body. We all have different roles, gifts, and assignments. Although they are not all the same roles, they are all equally important to accomplish the will of God. For the body to operate in unity, it will require being connected to one another. Therefore, staying in isolation will keep you out of God's will for your life. If Satan can grip you with enough fear, distrust, doubt, and hate, he has accomplished his mission of dividing and conquering. He uses those bad things that have happened to you to drive you to this place. You can't control the things that happened to you in the past. You aren't even responsible for some of those things, especially as a child. But you do have a responsibility to heal and work through it.

Stage 2: Codependence—In chapter 1, we discussed some codependent patterns. If you truly want to learn something about yourself, grab a sheet of paper or use the margins of this page, and list your name and the name of each difficult relationship you have experienced whether past or present. Beside each name, write which role you both held in the relationship. You may play different roles in different relationships. Once you have done this, notice which role you tend to assume the most. I encourage you to also jot down any patterns you identify about your part. If you felt fear in each relationship, write down what fear you felt.

It is important to understand that codependence is not love. It's a coping response for what feels necessary for emotional survival.

> For my father and my mother have forsaken me, But the LORD will take me up. Teach me Your way, LORD, And lead me on a level path Because of my enemies. Do not turn me over to the desire of my enemies, For false witnesses have risen against me, And the violent witness. I certainly believed that I would see the goodness of the LORD in the land of the living. Wait for the LORD; Be strong and let your heart take courage; Yes, wait for the LORD. (Psalm 27:10–14 NASB)

These verses address issues with parents, enemies, accusers, and abusers. But God will take you up, no matter what you have experienced! He is the only one who can fully heal the hurts that caused those fears in the first place. This verse also states why it is very important to wait for God to bring who you *need* in your life, not just someone to keep you from feeling lonely, unworthy, and abandoned.

The Bible warns of what to be watchful for and what to avoid.

> But realize this, that in the last days difficult times will come. For people will be lovers of self, lovers of money, boastful, arrogant, slanderers, disobedient to parents, ungrateful, unholy, unloving, irreconcilable, malicious gossips, without self-control, brutal, haters of good, treacherous, reckless, conceited, lovers of pleasure rather than lovers of God, holding to a form of godliness although they have denied its power; avoid such people as these. (2 Timothy 3:1–5 NASB)

Rushing into relationships often occurs when you see a form of godliness in someone and want to quickly assume this person is safe or sent from God. And to cure the lonely feeling you feel, we may throw all caution to the wind ignoring the other obvious warning signs. God isn't just issuing a warning and a command in these verses. He does so to let you know how to detect the behaviors in others that need healing too. It is very important to heal *before* engaging in close relationships with others so that you don't bring your past hurts into your present relationships, causing further damage to you or to them. The idea is for the relationship to be successful; one you can be grateful for and cherish. Maybe you have worked on these things already with therapy, counseling, or coaching, but that does not mean the person you are engaging with has put in the same work for themselves. God knows their heart; and if they are unhealthy for you in ways you can't always see, why would you *not* want to consult God before jumping in, knowing He sees what you can't?

Below are some questions to help grow your self-awareness.

1. How willing are you to engage with your family, friends, coworkers, support groups, and worship groups? Why or why not? If your willingness depends on the group, explain your reasoning toward each group.

2. What do you believe God is personally saying to you in Psalm 27:10–14?

3. Do you find it difficult to wait on God for anything? Why or why not?

4. Do you compromise warning signs when someone new comes into your life? Explain.

5. Do you do the same thing when someone from the past with whom you had an unhealthy relationship resurfaces in your life? Explain.

Searching and Fearless Inventory

And He has said to me, "My grace is sufficient for you, for power is perfected in weakness." Most gladly, therefore, I will rather boast about my weaknesses, so that the power of Christ may dwell in me.

—2 Corinthians 12:9 (NASB)

Step 4 in this relationship construction process is where you inventory past relationships, examining the hurt in order to grow. Before beginning, you first need to identify someone you trust and with whom you are comfortable, to support you during this process. This person should be someone who will not be judgmental. Step 5 will be a step where you actually share this inventory with this person. So be sure the person you have walking with you on this journey is the person you feel safe to share your inventory with when the time comes.

In this inventory, there are six areas of focus. These are

1. *Who* the relationship was with that is still impacting you today, whether through resentment, bitterness, fear, pain, lack of trust, etc.

2. *What* happened in the relationship?

3. *How* did the event impact you then?

4. *How* is the event still affecting you today?

5. What was *your part* in it? You don't always have to be a part of the hurt; however, this is where you must honestly look at your role to make sure you are not in denial in any way. Someone may have hurt you, and although you may not have done anything to cause it, and you may not have hurt them back, you very well may have hurt someone else in similar ways who had nothing to do with this particular event. Diligently search this section while praying that God reveals anything you need to see here.

6. List anyone *you have hurt* in the past and what the hurt was. These are the people toward whom you may not have any resentments and therefore don't already have them listed.

It's important to openly and honestly examine yourself to be sure you cover anything that could be hindering your peace. As you write your inventory, be sure to address each of the six areas above. The above key words are in *italics* to help you revisit the questions easily as you inventory each situation.

If the thought of this inventory feels difficult right now, take courage in scripture:

> "For I will restore you to health and I will heal you
> of your wounds," declares the LORD, "Because
> they have called you an outcast, saying: 'It is Zion;
> no one cares for her.'" (Jeremiah 30:17 NASB)

Pray and draw close to God as you go through this step. Each time you begin working on this inventory, begin and end in prayer.

I also suggest you end with scriptures that help lift your spirit each time. Below are some questions to help you prepare for the inventory. The page at the end of this section includes a list of scriptures that you may find beneficial on this journey.

1. What concerns do you have as you are preparing for this inventory?

2. What do you hope to get from this exercise?

3. Who have you identified as your safe person or sponsor to walk with through this part of your journey? Have you discussed it with this person? If not, when do you plan to do so?

Scriptures of Encouragement

The LORD is near to the brokenhearted And saves those who are crushed in spirit. (Psalm 34:18 NASB)

From my distress I called upon the LORD; The LORD answered me and put me in an open space. (Psalm 118:5 NASB)

He heals the brokenhearted And binds up their wounds. (Psalm 147:3 NASB)

Do not fear, for I am with you; Do not be afraid, for I am your God. I will strengthen you, I will also help you, I will also uphold you with My righteous right hand. (Isaiah 41:10 NASB)

Blessed are those who mourn, for they will be comforted. (Matthew 5:4 NASB)

Come to Me, all who are weary and burdened, and I will give you rest. (Matthew 11:28 NASB)

These things I have spoken to you so that in Me you may have peace. In the world you have tribulation, but take courage; I have overcome the world. (John 16:33 NASB)

It was for freedom that Christ set us free; therefore keep standing firm and do not be subject again to a yoke of slavery. (Galatians 5:1 NASB)

I can do all things through Him who strengthens me. (Philippians 4:13 NASB)

For God has not given us a spirit of timidity, but of power and love and discipline. (2 Timothy 1:7 NASB)

CHAPTER 5

Step 5

We admitted to ourselves, to God, and to another human being the exact nature of our wrongs.

> One who conceals his wrongdoings will not prosper, But one who confesses and abandons them will find compassion.
> —Proverbs 28:13 (NASB)

> Do not fear, for I am with you; Do not be afraid, for I am your God. I will strengthen you, I will also help you, I will also uphold you with my righteous right hand.
> —Isaiah 41:10 (NASB)

Sharing Is Healing

Once you have completed your moral inventory and have identified who you plan to share it with, it's time for the sharing to begin. The Bible tells us to confess for healing.

> Therefore, confess your sins to one another, and pray for one another so that you may be healed. A prayer of a righteous person, when it is brought about, can accomplish much. (James 5:16 NASB)

Sharing your experiences with someone is where freedom begins on the inside. There may be some things you have never shared with anyone, and it could be eating at you more than you realize. Sharing also helps you to step out of denial. Challenge yourself to be sure you are not holding back anything.

Sharing with someone may feel uncomfortable, but it is easier if you are truly sharing with someone whom you trust to maintain your privacy and won't judge you. Don't share your inventory with just anyone. If the person you plan to share your inventory with is also working on this program with you, it can be helpful to share some of your inventory back and forth to build a bond and level the field somewhat. If you share together, it is also important for that person to be what you need them to be for you: a nonjudgmental safe space for them to share with complete confidentiality.

> One who goes about as a slanderer reveals secrets,
> But one who is trustworthy conceals a matter.
> (Proverbs 11:13 NASB)

The goal of this step is to begin abandoning the hold these old things have over you to make space for new experiences. This is one abandonment that should bring you relief. To release this hold, you must be working toward an understanding of where and why the actions of yourself and others may have occurred.

For example, let's look at the first entry on your inventory. After sharing this entry, answer the following questions:

1. What do you know about this person's past hurt?

2. Did either of you possibly act on old unhealed wounds?

3. What basis can you find to consider forgiving them?

Separating the act that was committed from the individual who committed it is essential when working toward forgiveness. For example, have you ever hurt someone that you hoped would forgive you and not hold it against you as a person? I'm sure if we were all honest, we could identify a time when we needed this kind of forgiveness.

Forgiving someone doesn't mean you won't still experience triggers from the harm done. It doesn't mean you won't be reminded of it from time to time. When you forgive, forgive the act committed against you while giving grace to the person who committed it. It will loosen the hold it has had on you, your peace, and your life. If bitterness and resentment are the poison in your wound, then forgiveness is the ointment for healing it. Isn't that what Jesus did for you when He saved you? The Word of God tells us we need to give forgiveness in order to get forgiveness in Matthew 6:14.

Now is the time to meet with your safe person and share your inventory. Let the sharing begin!

> I prayed to the LORD my God and confessed, and said, "Oh, LORD, the great and awesome God, who keeps His covenant and faithfulness for those who love Him and keep His commandments, we have sinned, we have done wrong, and acted wickedly and rebelled, even turning aside from Your commandments and ordinances. (Daniel 9:4–5 NASB)

I encourage you to take a few moments to read Psalm 103:1–13 to experience God's grace over your life today.

> A Psalm of David. Bless the LORD, my soul, And all that is within me, bless His holy name. Bless the LORD, my soul, And do not forget any of his benefits; Who pardons all your guilt, Who heals all your diseases; Who redeems your life from the pit, Who crowns you with favor and compassion; Who satisfies your years with good things, So that your youth is renewed like the eagle. The LORD performs righteous deeds And judgments for all who are oppressed. He

made known His ways to Moses, His deeds to the sons of Israel. The LORD is compassionate and gracious, Slow to anger and abounding in mercy. He will not always contend with us, Nor will He keep His anger forever. He has not dealt with us according to our sins, Nor rewarded us according to our guilty deeds. For as high as the heavens are above the earth, So great is His mercy toward those who fear Him. As far as the east is from the west, So far has He removed our wrongdoings from us. Just as a father has compassion on his children, So the LORD has compassion on those who fear Him.

Below are some questions that may help make sharing easier.

1. What concerns do you have about sharing your inventory with someone else?

2. Describe a time you hurt someone and they continued to hold it against you. How does that impact you today?

3. After sharing your inventory and answering the three questions leading to forgiveness, is there anyone whom you still find hard to forgive in your inventory? Explain.

4. Have you forgiven yourself of any part you believe you had in the situations on your inventory? Why or why not?

5. Do you believe God has forgiven you for any part you may have had which hurt someone else? If not, have you prayed and asked Him to? If not, why not?

CHAPTER 6

Step 6

We became entirely ready to have God remove any fear of abandonment, along with the belief that we are not enough for ourselves, for God, or for others.

> The LORD is for me; I will not fear; What can man do to me?
>
> —Psalm 118:6 (NASB)

> For you were called to freedom, brothers and sisters; only do not turn your freedom into an opportunity for the flesh, but serve one another through love.
>
> —Galatians 5:13 (NASB)

Who Do I Want to Be?

Hopefully, you've now learned where some of your thoughts and emotions have been coming from through the inventory process. I hope you also feel a great deal of weight off you now to make more room for something new.

In developing your character, you must first decide who you want to be. Start by examining your morals and values. Morals and values are two terms so repeatedly intertwined that it's easy to automatically assume values equal good qualities like morals do. However, your current values may not be aligned with who you want to be at this point.

Values form around your experiences. For example, has someone ever lied to you and it hurt? Then because of that, you may have a top value of honesty, which is a good value. Then there are other times when people value things like pride, money, or power, which also come from ideals and experiences. The Bible is clear about the dangers of pride, money, and power. They may seem good to the person in the moment and in this life, but at what cost? Holding true to these types of values won't bring you fulfillment or joy. They generally exist because of fear. I know that may not make sense to you now, but pride is triggered when you feel attacked or threatened. It's also exerted when you lack self-confidence to mask those insecurities. Valuing money generally comes from a fear of not having it. Some have a dependency on money for security. Once again, fear of not having it can make it valuable to you. Power is no different. Power seekers are searching for control. Why do you feel the need to control something if you don't fear what could happen if you weren't in control? If you deal with your fears, then you can replace your values with other values based on Christ's likeness.

I challenge you to identify your top five values. Those top five values will tend to flare up feelings of frustration or even anger when someone violates them. Pay attention to this. Your anger may just reveal your true values. For example, when someone's talk doesn't match their walk, it tends to anger me. Therefore, integrity is one of my top values.

It's important to take an honest look at your values. Don't just pick what feels good or what you believe they should be. Honestly identify what things you defend the most for whatever reason.

When you violate your own values, feelings of shame tend to arise rather than anger. It's important to work through those things quickly. The idea is to acknowledge it. Examine why you violated them to learn from it going forward and forgive yourself for the violation. Everybody makes mistakes. The Bible tells us that no one is without sin or mistakes. But holding on to unforgiveness toward yourself is just as unproductive as holding on to unforgiveness toward someone else, if not more. Always look for the lesson so that the next time the same or similar situation arises, you can recall what you've learned to hopefully not repeat it again. But if you do, keep looking for the lesson and patterns. You will eventually catch your triggers early enough to respond differently in those moments.

Try answering the following questions as a point of inspection about your relationship with yourself.

1. At this moment, how do you currently feel about yourself? Is this outlook beginning to improve as you reconstruct your relationship with yourself? Explain.

2. What kind of relationship do you want to have with yourself? How do you *want* to feel about yourself?

3. What do you believe are your top five values today? How well do you uphold them?

4. What steps do you need to take to grow toward who you want to be?

5. What obstacles might you face in becoming who you want to be and why? Your answer to this question is a good indicator of where you may need boundaries for yourself. We place boundaries around things we value. This is why you need self-forgiveness and self-worth. You won't protect what you resent, including yourself. You

are worth protecting! And no one but God and you are necessarily going to protect you. We will discuss more on boundaries in another chapter.

6. Do you believe you are worth boundaries? Why or why not?

7. What is the hardest part for you in setting boundaries for yourself?

Now What?

> Therefore, having been justified by faith, we have peace with God through our Lord Jesus Christ, through whom we also have obtained our introduction by faith into this grace in which we stand; and we celebrate in hope of the glory of God. And not only this, but we also celebrate in our tribulations, knowing that tribulation brings about perseverance; and perseverance, proven character; and proven character, hope; and hope does not disappoint, because the love of God has been poured out within our hearts through the Holy Spirit who was given to us.
>
> —Romans 5:1–5 (NASB)

It's time to begin strengthening your relationship with God. This step is about combatting the fear of abandonment. There is no guarantee in life that people won't one day leave you, whether by choice, by passing away, or because you find that your life is moving in different directions. There is no guarantee that you will always be able to stay in your comfort zone to minimize fear either. People will come and go. Circumstances will always be changing.

Having a relationship with God, which goes beyond knowing and believing in Him, is the key to breaking a fear of abandonment. It goes beyond receiving His forgiveness for sins, too. This will be the most important relationship you will ever form because it is the only relationship that you can count on never leaving you or forsaking you. You may walk away from Him from time to time, but He will always be right where you left Him, waiting for you to call out to Him.

Great relationships require time and effort, no matter what kind of relationship it is. You may like to hear about the love, forgiveness, and grace God has to offer. The part you may not always look at is that He wants you to actually live for Him. Many of His promises in the Bible have a portion of it that people don't always quote. It's the part of the verse that says if you do *this,* God will do *that.* Look at this particular verse for an example:

> If you remain in Me, and My words remain in you, ask whatever you wish, and it will be done for you. (John 15:7 NASB)

It's easy to put expectations on God because His word says He will do whatever you ask in His name. Then, when God doesn't deliver, it's also easy to hold it against Him and allow yourself to become angry. What you should do instead is read the entire scripture and examine whether you were doing your part. Have you been *remaining* in Jesus? If not, maybe the move of God's hand is waiting on your repentance. He will always make good on His promises to His children in His time, but you must do your part. To remain in Jesus means to continually seek His will, His direction, and His grace, allowing yourself to be transformed into His image by becoming more Christlike.

There is another scenario where God tends to get the blame. When you make choices and decisions without consulting His direction, and then expect Him to cosign the things He didn't want you to do in the first place, you can wrongly place blame on Him when it doesn't work out like you hoped it would.

Once you have been saved by His grace, which is free to you and something you don't have to earn, He desires a real relationship with you. Are you embracing the opportunity to build this relationship? It's easy to want the benefits of His love, forgiveness, and His offer to spend eternity with Him in Heaven. If it's hard for you to live for God now, how will you be able to live for Him in eternity?

Living for God does not look like perfection. It's loving Him enough to be willing to grow more Christlike. Jesus says, "If you love Me, you will keep My commandments," (John 14:15 NASB). If you have ever said the words to someone, "If you love me you wouldn't do that to me," how is your expectation of love any different from Jesus's? It isn't.

As with any healthy relationship, a relationship with Jesus requires communication, effort, and time. It's about caring enough to learn His character. He is always available for communication. He will commit more effort than you ever possibly could, even at your best efforts. He will give His time to you as much as you give your time to Him. This is one relationship you can't rightfully blame the other party for not showing up or caring about you. If you don't have a deep relationship with Him, it's only because you choose not to.

Do you believe you are enough for God? Whether you believe it or not, I'll answer that for you. Yes, you are! Not only did God send His Son, Jesus, to take your place and die for your sins, He didn't stop there in His plans for you.

> Do you not know that you are a temple of God and that the Spirit of God dwells in you? (1 Corinthians 3:16 NASB)

When you are saved by His grace, Christ dwells in you, which is why your body is referred to as temple. And no matter how you treat that temple, it won't change the fact that God cares for it. Self-care is important. If your home or church needs repairs, would you not repair it? These bodily temples are no different. Self-care works the same way.

> Have I not commanded you? Be strong and courageous! Do not be terrified nor dismayed, for the LORD your God is with you wherever you go. (Joshua 1:9 NASB)

All the time spent feeling alone, and yet you are never alone. You just don't necessarily know the one in the room with you intimately enough to trust His presence is there. If you do know Him, you either don't think to call on Him, or you may prefer self-reliance and control.

The Bible tells you just how much care He took in making you.

> For You created my innermost parts; You wove me in my mother's womb. I will give thanks to You, because I am awesomely and wonderfully made; Wonderful are Your works, And my soul knows it very well. (Psalm 139:13–14 NASB)

God has plans for you. And not just any plans. These are plans you don't want to miss!

> "For I know the plans that I have for you," declares the LORD, "plans for prosperity and not for disaster, to give you a future and a hope." (Jeremiah 29:11 NASB)

To sum up just how much you are enough for God and how He so desires a relationship with you, let's finish out that scripture in Jeremiah:

> Then you will call upon Me and come and pray to Me, and I will listen to you. And you will seek Me and find Me when you search for Me with all your heart. I will let Myself be found by you … (Jeremiah 12:14 NASB)

I hope you are starting to see just how much God loves you and that you are enough for Him. The question now is this: Is He enough for you?

Try answering the following questions:

1. Do you believe God is with you everywhere you go? Why or why not?

2. God made you in His image for great works. What do you believe God had in mind about you when He created you? Be specific.

3. Do you focus more energy on living your life the here and now, or do you focus more on living today for eternity? Explain.

4. Do you believe the scripture in Jeremiah 29:11? Why or why not? Do you ever ask God about what plans He has for you? Has He shown you yet?

Enough for Others: Who Decides?

> And coming to Him as to a living stone which has been rejected by people, but is choice and precious in the sight of God.
>
> —1 Peter 2:4 (NASB)

Do you avoid *good* relationships because you wonder if you are good enough for them? The good part is that others don't get to decide. You do. If you're questioning your worth because people seem to keep walking away, it's not about being good enough. It's about differences, such as whether characters and values align, and if the direction you each have for your lives is compatible. The fact that these things may be different does not mean you're not good enough or that the relationship is bad. There are just differences between you. Sometimes you can overcome those things, and other times you are just too far apart to come together. It isn't realistic to think that differences somehow mean you or they are unworthy. Differences do not equal self valuation.

Codependence causes people to operate on feelings and emotions more than logic and reasoning. Loneliness, fear, and people-pleasing can feel like the loudest voice in the relationship when codependence is present. In 2 Timothy 1:7, you will find great wisdom and direction in dealing with feelings of rejection. Notice how this verse explains that God has *not* given you a spirit of timidity, or fear. He gave you a spirit of power, love, and discipline, or as some versions state a sound mind. To tap into that spirit, lean into God and simply including Him.

Together, God and you can safely determine who the "others" should be in your life without fear. If you have to worry about whether someone or something is right for you or not, stop and ask yourself who or what are you putting your trust in to see to the outcome? If it is anything besides God, you have reason to worry. People, even on their best day will fail you, even when they don't mean to. We are human, not perfection. But having a solid relationship with God ensures you won't face disappointment alone, nor have to sit in less self-worth because of it. That in itself helps to remove the fear of the what-ifs in relationships.

If you want a different result, you must do something different. Let's start by trading the codependent patterns in for a healthy pattern, the way we were designed to relate.

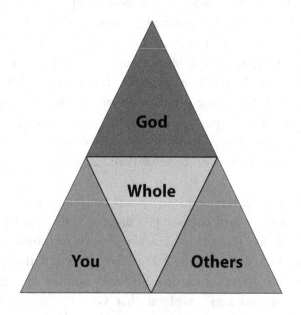

Notice in this diagram, there are no codependent roles or labels. It's just God, you, and others. When your relationship is so strong with God that you value His input enough to prevent old patterns from returning, you *want* to seek His guidance about who you should form relationships with: from friends, business partners, romantic relationships, etc. Remember, when you enter a relationship with others in mind first, you tend to be second, and God may not even get invited to the party. Seeking wisdom from the Holy Spirit about any relationship is a key to breaking old cycles.

It is easy to get swept up by the newness and excitement of a new friendship or romantic relationship. You may be concerned that if you ask God if this is part of his plan, He might reveal that this relationship is *not* for you. Would you overlook His guidance if so and continue the relationship? Or do you choose to not even ask God, especially if feelings are now involved? God isn't the parent you have to get permission from to go out on a date. He gives you freewill to choose the things you do. He is, however, the safest best friend you will ever have who knows more than you do about the situation, the future, and the things you do not know. He is a Heavenly Father who loves His children so much, that He wants good things for them. Involving Him will either give you a peace in moving forward in the relationship or clarity about reasons this might not be for you. At the end of the day, the choice is still yours. Praying for signs to be revealed and the wisdom to recognize them will help you see what you need to see. The goal is not to have more codependent relationships full of chaos and worry, but to have healthy relationships that contain trust, respect, and a sound-mind, all of which are components of a relationship where you can just *be*.

Below are more questions to help you keep the relational building process going:

1. Is it hard to ask for and accept God's direction about your relationships? Why or why not?

2. Before this chapter, did you see your differences from others as a potential form of rejection? Why or why not?

3. Is it hard for you to accept and let go of people when necessary? Explain.

4. What do you need to do differently to get different results as people come into your life going forward?

5. At what point do you usually talk to God about a relationship? How has that been working for you?

CHAPTER 7

Step 7

We humbly asked Him to remove anything that hinders us from being our true self in His image.

> Therefore be imitators of God, as beloved children; and walk in love, just as Christ also loved you and gave Himself up for us, an offering and a sacrifice to God as a fragrant aroma.
>
> —Ephesians 5:1–2 (NASB)

> For God has not given us a spirit of timidity, but of power and love and discipline.
>
> —2 Timothy 1:7 (NASB)

Where Are My Boundaries?

One factor that seems to impact the success of any relationship is the pace at which it grows. Moving too fast is like running into a building that may look good on the outside but is burning down on the inside. And once you get inside, you find it hard to get out. If you wait until too many emotions are involved before evaluating whether or not this is a healthy place for you and/or the other person, you may find it much harder to escape. You could save yourself a lot of potential hurt and struggle if you would take the time to assess the situation logically before emotions get involved.

Some things to watch for in any relationship are the character traits being shown. Are the things they say they value actually reflected in their actions? Do their paths or plans align with yours, if considering a romantic relationship or a business relationship?

Let's talk about trust. If someone shares gossip, there could be trust issues. If a person breaks trust with someone else, they may break trust with you. How a person treats other people is a good indication of how they will treat you. How do they treat their family and/or the people they are closest to? If disrespectfully, then guess what? Falling in love with you may just make you a target for being disrespected as well.

It's time to discuss boundaries. It amazes me how many people shudder at the mention of this word. The idea of setting boundaries can be extremely challenging, especially for people pleasers. There is one thing you eventually have to decide: Are you going to protect your mental, physical, emotional, and spiritual well-being, or are you going to protect that person's opinion of you out of fear? You don't generally get to do both. Let me give you another perspective on boundaries that may just help you actually value them rather than fear them.

Here's the scene: Imagine you live on a vacant square lot in a subdivision in town. The people you are closest to are your neighbors. Each one has their own square lot surrounding yours. You have one to the right, one to the left, one to the back of your lot, and a few across the street. Your lot represents the space in your life where you live and reside. How you protect your space is how safe you will remain.

You may trust people very little and live in such fear that you build walls around your property. These walls can be so high no one can see over them, nor can you see out. You isolate yourself in this space, only leaving it in have-to situations.

On the other hand, you may have wide open spaces with no fences so as to let anyone or anything come and go in your yard. This includes people, things, habits, etc. You may fear that if you don't let the person keep coming over who hurts you every time they show up, they may think you don't love them. You'll feel like you're being mean to them. If they get upset, they may never come back. But they hurt you practically every time they show up. The problem is not that they might walk away and never come back. Fear that if they don't come back, nobody else will either is the root issue. So you make your space as easy as possible to access in case someone, anyone, will show up. You'll do anything to not be alone.

I literally had a girl tell me once that bad love was better than no love at all. Think about that: Is abuse better than loneliness? If your answer is yes, then your struggle isn't with loneliness. It's with value in yourself. People protect what they value. If you're not willing to protect yourself and what is in your best interest, you have yet to see you are worth protecting. You are valued and loved by the One who created you! If this is you, I encourage you to read the scriptures daily about just how much God loves you. Pray that He helps you feel His love until you start protecting you and your space.

Now, if you are starting to believe you are enough and worthy of healthy connections with God and others, it's time to learn how to set boundaries you actually welcome into your life. After all, if you are working on healing, you have something worth protecting.

Let's stay with this same scene. Imagine you are back on your square lot that you've worked hard to get. You've cleaned it up and dug the dirt to build a foundation based on healing and growth. You hopefully have allowed God to be the foundation building block for your home. But while you are building that house, you see trash from other yards blowing over into yours. You keep picking it up, but it's back the next day. Old you who doesn't want to risk offending anyone will just go out there and clean up the trash that other people either dumped on your yard or that blew over from the wind. Then the people start to come over to your yard and hang out, doing and saying things you have worked hard to break for yourself. The next day, you go grab your fencing materials you've had in storage for a long time, knowing you need to put up a fence, but you've been too afraid of what the neighbors will say or think.

You begin putting up your fence. As you do, some of your closest friends and family are walking by asking what you're doing and why. You begin sharing about the work you've been doing in your space and how you want to protect it. They may commend you at first and tell you how proud they are for you, until it starts to affect the free pass they've had to your yard up to this point. They congratulate you and keep walking to let you work because they haven't felt the effects of it yet.

You set the corner posts. These posts are the anchors for your space. They represent the things you have started doing regularly that keep you growing, healthy, and connected to God. Maybe one of them is prayer each morning. Maybe one is journaling. Maybe one is attending a weekly support group or worship group. Maybe one is reading your Bible daily. These are examples of how the things that are growing you do not need to be compromised or forgotten. The minute you stop doing them, you jeopardize your growth. Anyone that comes into your space to hinder your growth, tempt you, or disrespect your boundaries may actually cause you setbacks. They may even start to speak negatively about this new you. These are the people who need to remain on the other side of the fence. Just because others choose not to grow doesn't mean you stunt your own growth to please them.

Undoubtedly when they drop by to visit using the same old tactics to get you to let your guard down in the past, and you tell them you won't (not can't) be around that anymore, the boundary pushing will begin. The manipulation, the guilt trips, the begging, etc. are tactics to get you to compromise your boundaries. They are used to your yard not having any fences and they may have gotten away with more in your space in the past. You may even hear things like, "You think you are going to tell me no now? You can't control me. You can't tell me what to do." They are right. You can't. And herein lies the misconception of boundaries.

A boundary is not about telling the other person what they can or can't do. It's establishing what *you* will and won't do anymore. Boundaries are for your protection, not for you to control other people. People have the freedom to do whatever they want, just not in your yard. Not inside your fence. This is where the battle of self begins. You need the strength and power of the Holy Spirit especially as you learn to guard your gate from those that don't respect or support the healed version of you. This is where you learn who's been in your life because they genuinely love you and who has been using and abusing you without any resistance.

Are we talking about actual lots and houses here? No. Your house is you. Your yard is the place where you abide. It's your immediate safe space.

The new you no longer lives in your old abandoned house anymore! You are building a new house with a solid foundation, even if you and God are the only two dwelling there. You'll have the greatest gift on earth … peace! During this construction phase, it's amazing how your people, places, and things start to change. Your growth draws likeminded people to you like a moth to a flame, who also want to grow and heal. You find yourself becoming an inspiration to others longing for the strength, peace, and self-worth you've found. All the while, you begin to lean into the discernment of the Holy Spirit for who is safe to be in your space and who might need to stay on the other side of the fence.

The thing about fences is that you are not shutting people out of your life like they might accuse you of doing. You can meet people at a fence. You can talk to them at a safe distance and when it's safe to do so. You can share what worked for you to heal when they get ready to heal themselves. But your peace and joy will radiate over that fence until they crave what you have found or what their life is missing. It's almost like tough love. Sometimes the best gift you will ever give someone is to stop pleasing them, thus, driving them to look inwardly at themselves. If they are ever going to see the truth about what their life is missing, they first have to step out of denial just like you have done. It's hard for someone to see what they need when people still cater to their every demand and desire. No matter what accusations they may throw your way, if you know the truth about yourself and the truth about how much God loves and cares for you, then any accusation or judgment they may throw at you doesn't apply. Toss it out. It's an attempt to get you to tear that fence down and let them in. Hold fast to God. The Holy Spirit will help you guard your gate and protect you when others try pressing your boundaries. But you will have to face it. Some people you may have to love from a distance. Maybe one day, they will find their own healing and then you can be closer again.

In new relationships, you won't always recognize codependence quickly. And if you do, you won't necessarily know how much work they may have done on themselves. Take your time to observe and get to know one another. Learn one another's values and boundaries up front. If you respect each other's boundaries and values while remaining true to your own, there will be a lot less to undo later. Use 1 Corinthians 13 verses of what love is and is not as your guide.

If you're going to be equally yoked in a romantic relationship that one day you hope to turn into marriage, you need to consider many more topics, such as beliefs, children, faith, finances, future plans with careers, etc. If your lives are not on the same page, talk to God about it. Only God knows if this person is who He has for you or not.

Let's talk about the biblical design for marriage. Two people become one person. You are still individuals, but what you do and what your spouse does affects the other one. There is no way around that. You are one. This is why it is important to be equally yoked.

A yoke is a wooden rectangular plank of wood that had two notches cut out of it at the bottom for the plank to rest on the necks of two oxen. These oxen were tied together side by side with this plank of wood. They were then a team used to haul things on a wagon, plow a field, or some other job. What one of them did, the other had to do. There were also reigns attached to the plank for the guide to lead this pair of oxen.

So what does this have to do with healthy relationships? Let's look at a few verses to explain.

> Do not be bound together with unbelievers; for what partnership have righteousness with lawlessness, or what fellowship has light with darkness?
> —2 Corinthians 6:14 (NASB)

Then Jesus says the following:

> Take My yoke upon you and learn from Me, for
> I am gentle and humble in heart, and *you will find*
> *rest for your souls*. For My yoke is easy and My
> burden is light. (Matthew 11:29–30 NASB)

Why would you *not* want to involve Jesus in your relationships with this kind of promise? In a marriage, you should be accepted, loved, cherished, encouraging to one another, and operating as a true team. Wearing your own yoke rather than the one Jesus has for you, is a yoke of slavery. It will leave you feeling trapped and frustrated, and it won't always fit. If you are determined to wear your own yoke that you chose and made yourself, then you can't wear it and hold the reigns at the same time. Just imagine all the struggle that comes with this kind of relationship.

> It was for freedom that Christ set us free; therefore
> keep standing firm and do not be subject again to
> a yoke of slavery. (Galatians 5:1 NASB)

I hope you are starting to see just how important it is to know yourself and what God says about you. I hope you long for a relationship with Jesus so deeply that there is no way you want to enter a relationship without Him being at the center. I hope you value your growth enough that you will protect it with necessary boundaries, defining what you will and will not have in your life. I hope your relationship is so strong with Jesus that you only want the Holy Spirit holding the reigns of your life and your future in His hands.

I'll leave you with this thought as we complete this particular step: We teach others how to treat us by the way we treat ourselves.

If you tear your fence down, you've taught them that your boundaries have less value than their desires. If you won't protect yourself, how can you expect them to? This is a pivotal moment, a perspective shift. I encourage you to develop a plan of action for challenges you anticipate so that you are not caught off guard when they occur. You will be prepared to respond rather than react. Things you are hopefully looking to keep out of your space are abusive cycles, old habits that pull you away from God, or any addictive behaviors that are temptations to you at this point in your life, placing this person on the throne of your life rather than God being on your throne, etc. Remember, boundaries are not to isolate you or shut you off from the world. It's guiding principles to help you engage with others healthily. It's about how you want to live on your lot.

Below are some questions to help you start thinking about the safety of your space.

1. What do you look for in a friendship as far as a person's character, values, etc.?

2. What do you look for in a person with whom you are considering having a romantic relationship?

3. How much time do you spend getting to know someone before committing to the relationship? Do you think your time frame is enough? Why or why not?

4. How do you know when you are compatible with someone in a relationship?

5. What are you prepared to allow God to help you remove from your space? Be specific.

6. What do you plan to replace these things with? Be specific.

7. Boundaries only work if you are prepared to let go of people who choose to walk out of your life because they aren't where you are now. How do you plan to replace your fear of people leaving?

8. What boundaries do you recognize need to be set for your space? How will you set them?

9. In detail, describe some situations you anticipate will challenge you to tear your fence down and compromise all of the things that keep you growing and healthy. What will be the hardest part of the moment? What do you envision yourself doing to protect your healthy space?

CHAPTER 8

Step 8

We made a list of all persons we had harmed and became willing to make amends to them all.

> But now you also, rid yourselves of all of them: anger, wrath, malice, slander, and obscene speech from your mouth. Do not lie to one another, since you stripped off the old self with its evil practices, and have put on the new self, which is being renewed to a true knowledge according to the image of the One who created it.
>
> (Colossians 3:8–10 NASB)

> For if you forgive others for their transgressions, your heavenly Father will also forgive you.
>
> —Matthew 6:14 (NASB)

Are You Willing?

Step 8 is about recognizing that there are still some situations, no matter how much time has passed, that deserve an apology for the hurt you may have caused to someone involved. Undoubtedly, you can't just go to some of those people at this point because it might damage their lives now. You also can't open doors back up that could still be harmful to you like in abuse cases, for example. And some people may have passed away at this point. We will discuss more about how to handle these situations in the next chapter. For now, you are only identifying who you actually owe amends.

To identify the people you owe this to, go back to your moral inventory in chapter 4. Search your heart about this and pray for discernment over each one. This could be for the harm you caused to them or it could be how you retaliated after the way they hurt you. And if you're thinking, "I'm not apologizing to them because they never apologized to me for how they hurt me," it doesn't matter. If you truly want to live a Christlike life in freedom from all the old resentments, you must prepare your heart to apologize for your part, even if they don't. This is *only* about cleaning up your side of the street.

If anyone in the world ever had the right to hold a grudge against anyone by man's standards, it was Jesus. He had more haters, more slurs, more abuse, more name-calling, and yet He prayed God would forgive them anyway. He prayed for his enemies. Yes, it is Jesus, and He is perfect in all of His ways. But He gave His life for you and will forgive you the same way He forgave his haters. Don't you think it's time to forgive others you resent too? Jesus teaches us this:

> For if you forgive other people for their offenses, your heavenly Father will also forgive you. (Matthew 6:14 NASB)

This is not the point you rush over to everyone's house or begin calling them to say you're sorry. This is just the identification step. There are preparations to be made first. As you review your inventory, if someone you feel you owe an amend has passed away, still include them on your list.

It's easy to focus on the areas you need to clean up while still holding on to bitterness and resentments you just aren't ready and willing to forgive. Whether or not you are ready to extend mercy and grace, it's time to identify those you need to forgive as well. Unforgiveness will take from you everything that receiving forgiveness gives to you. Bitterness and resentment can consume you so much that your heart, mind, soul, and spirit are all affected negatively. It will eventually bleed onto others you care about. This process is about restoring joy and peace in all areas of your life. And when you forgive someone, it sets you free, whether it sets them free or not in their own heart and mind. It loses the hold it's had over you.

Have you ever had someone forgive you before you ever apologized to them? If you are like me, it always made me feel worse because

I saw the peace they had and knew I had no part in them finding that peace. I just had to sit in guilt and live with what I did, until I apologized anyway.

Sometimes the person you need to forgive is yourself. Not forgiving yourself is just as unproductive to your growth as anything else. If God has forgiven you, whether the person has forgiven you or not, you have no valid reason to not forgive yourself. Learn from it. Move forward by taking the lesson you've gained out of it and applying the lesson to your future. Below are some questions to consider when identifying amends to be made and forgiveness to be given.

1. How do you gauge whether or not you owe someone amends?

2. What is something difficult for you to forgive and why?

3. Do you have any fears as you consider forgiving someone on your inventory? Explain.

CHAPTER 9

Step 9

We made direct amends to such people whenever possible, except when doing so would injure them or others.

> So, as those who have been chosen of God, holy and beloved, put on a heart of compassion, kindness, humility, gentleness, and patience; bearing with one another, and forgiving each other, whoever has a complaint against anyone; just as the Lord forgave you, so must you do also.
>
> —Colossians 3:12–13 (NASB)

> For if you forgive others for their transgressions, your heavenly Father will also forgive you.
>
> —Matthew 6:14 (NASB)

When God Says Go

This is the amends step which is a pivotal moment. By now, you should have identified who you need to apologize to and who you still need to forgive. This is also the point where you might feel yourself trying to downplay the situation or searching for reasons not to follow through. You may even believe that forgiving the person somehow makes what they did seem OK. This is not the case. This is to free you. Also, if you begin to feel pride rising up inside as you prepare to make these amends, it is highly possible that you fear something worth protecting underneath your pride. Journaling can help pinpoint what those fears might be. If you address the fear, then the pride will melt away.

This is the point to begin very prayerfully seeking God's direction about who to make amends and how. Amends may be verbal, written, or in the form of living amends.

Verbal amends are good to make whenever possible. But some circumstances are not safe to do so. Similar concerns may apply to written amends as well. Whether you can approach this person or not, at minimum, I encourage you to write a letter to say what you would say if you could, just to release it from yourself.

That doesn't mean you have to give it to them if it isn't safe. You can, however, share the letter with the person you shared your inventory with in chapter 5. It helps to read those letters to a trusted person because the Bible tells us in James 5:16 that confessing to one another brings healing. It also gives you the opportunity to at least feel heard by someone even if it isn't the person you owe it to. This also applies for those you needed to apologize to who have already passed away. Writing a letter to someone who is now gone can help bring closure.

A living amends is when you truly repent, which means to turn and do the opposite, and living out that amends through the rest of your life, not hurting them or anyone else the same way again. For example, if you can't change what happened or apologize for it, you can repent to God, seeking forgiveness as with any sin. Then just don't repeat the hurt in the future to anyone else.

Prayerfully ask God who, when, and how to make each apology, and wait on His timing. This is not a step to be rushed or forced. You should act on these at the pace God leads you to. You will know when the time is right if you include Him in this process. Pray for the Holy Spirit to guard your heart and mind at the time of the amends and for their heart to be prepared to receive it.

One thing to examine before you make amends is to be certain you aren't having any expectations of the outcome. You shouldn't expect to hear "I forgive you" because they may not be prepared to forgive yet. You also can't expect to receive an apology back for the part they played in the situation that hurt you. They may not be in a place to apologize to you yet. After all, they may not be working on themselves the same way you chose to. It is *only* for you to clean up your side of the situation.

You should also be prepared to hear some hard things back. Sometimes people have held hurt inside for so long that the moment you go to make the amends, they may spew how that hurt made them feel. It will be hard to hear, but pray through it and remind yourself why you are doing this: to be free. Once you have apologized, whether they forgive you or not is between them and God. Your part is done. Just share what is in your heart without making excuses for your actions or pointing any kind of blame at anyone else. If you find yourself making statements such as, "I apologize for doing that to you, *but* ...," then you aren't ready. There needs to be no *but* statements following your apology.

Now let's move on to forgiveness. You won't always go to someone and tell them you forgave them. Some people may obviously not be safe for you to contact. It's actually forgiving them whether they ever know it or not. Until you forgive, it will eat at you deeply. There have been situations in my own life where I was not able to forgive until one of two things happened: I found empathy for them, or I related what they did to me to how I have hurt someone else similarly in the past.

Finding empathy can be hard to do, but it begins with what you know about them and about pain. People who have experienced hurt sometimes end up hurting other people the same way. They don't mean to necessarily. Just because someone has been hurt does not give them the right to hurt you or anyone else. We all have a responsibility to heal. But sometimes people don't know how to get the help they need or have not been afforded the opportunity to receive help. Left to deal with it alone, they sometimes project that pain to others in a similar way.

What do you know about the person who hurt you? Have you ever hurt someone the same way they hurt you? If you find empathy difficult, and you are still very hurt and angry, I challenge you to pray for God to heal them the way you want Him to heal you until you actually mean it. Just keep praying it anyway and watch what God does to change your heart toward forgiveness! Consider the following questions:

1. Do you have feelings of pride and/or fear at this moment about any of your amends? Explain.

2. Which amends do you think will be the hardest for you to make and why?

3. Which amends to make are you uncertain about? Explain.

4. How is holding on to unforgiveness affecting you?

5. Have you hurt someone in the past the same way anyone has hurt you? Explain.

6. Have you ever hoped someone would forgive you for something, but they refuse to? How has that affected you?

CHAPTER 10

Step 10

We continue taking personal inventory and when we are wrong, we promptly admit it, so that we keep our relationship with God, self, and others free and at peace.

> If possible, so far as it depends on you,
> be at peace with all people.
> —Romans 12:18 (NASB)

Do not get upset because of evildoers.
Do not be envious of wrongdoers. For
they will wither quickly like the grass,
And decay like the green plants. Trust
in the LORD and do good; Live in the
land and cultivate faithfulness. Delight
yourself in the LORD; And He will give
you the desires of your heart. Commit
your way to the LORD, Trust also in Him,
and He will do it.

—Psalm 37:1–5 (NASB)

Cleaning House

Step 10 in this reconstruction process is about taking out the trash and remaining responsible. It's known as daily inventory. If done properly and with commitment, it will transform how you handle your day-to-day life going forward. If this step is neglected, it will impact all three relationship categories you've worked hard to develop: your relationship with yourself, with God, and with other people. It's how you maintain peace on a day-to-day basis. Keep in mind that peace does not mean problem free. It's about the anchor holding us during the storms of life.

Let's paint the picture. Let's say it's 7:00 a.m. and you're driving to work. All of a sudden, someone cuts in front of you, and you spiral into a fit of road rage. Maybe road rage has been a long-time habit of yours, so you think nothing of it. But God sees it.

You get to work late, and your boss comes to you right away with a task he needs done by noon. This was unexpected, and you've already lost valuable time from doing your own work when you arrived late. Now, you have to drop your own work to dive hard into this task for your boss. You're frustrated and angry that he didn't tell you yesterday about the project because you would have made it a point to arrive early this morning to finish it. At this point, you've accumulated several bags of trash: the road rage, being late, and now being frustrated at your boss's lack of concern for your time.

You work frantically to get the task done and believe you've done a good job on it. You get to your boss by 11:55 a.m., just before the deadline, and he tells you that you've done it wrong. You've got to change some things about it and quick! You are so angry because no one apparently trained you properly from the beginning, or you would have done it correctly. However, you make the corrections quickly and turn it in, only to carry back with you another bag of trash toward the way you feel about your boss right now.

You go to lunch at the restaurant down the street to get away from the office for a few minutes and decompress. When you get your order, the waiter brings you the wrong food. You've already waited a long time and can't wait any longer for the cook to correct it. So you settle for something you didn't want and get it to go because you don't need to be late getting back. So much for decompressing. Not only did you bring that unwanted meal back with you to the office, but you also brought another bag of trash from being so frustrated that no one seems to get anything right anymore!

At this point, your afternoon is spent doing routine work. You are just waiting for quitting time so you can go home and forget about this day. About fifteen minutes from closing, you are told your help is needed on a problem that's arisen, which will cause you to work late. Although flattered that they need your help, once again, you don't get to leave and spend your evening the way you wanted to. And it came with another bag of trash for once again infringing on your time.

While working on the problem, you yelled at your coworker out of frustration for something that wasn't their fault. They snapped back, and now you're mad at the comment they just made, even though you know you deserved it. Rather than apologizing, you get offended because they called you out on your behavior. Two more bags of trash are now going home with you. Looks like you're going to need a pickup truck to haul all of this trash home that you've accumulated throughout the day.

You finally get to leave for the evening. On the way home, you notice the drive isn't so bad because rush-hour traffic has had time to get ahead of you. One scenario of how the evening plays out is that you blame this day on just being a bad day and tomorrow will hopefully be better. You just want to go home and go to bed. When you get home, you have to take all of the trash in with you because you haven't dealt with it yet. You get to your bed and realize you can't sleep. You can't get comfortable because there are so many bags of trash on your mind from the day, not to mention still feeling stressed out and angry. You tossed and turned all night dreading the alarm clock going off because honestly, you just aren't ready to face another day. You stuff the trash down, get up, and begin your day anyway. You still have to load all of that trash up to take with you on your ride to work and throughout your day because you have yet to deal with it. It's weighing you down and taking all of your motivation with it.

This is what life looks like without daily inventory. The more days that pass by, the more bags of trash you have blocking you from attaining peace. Not only that, but you now have a huge wall of trash between you and God and between you and your family, friends, and coworkers. You lose your joy in life, feeling trapped, boxed in, and isolated.

Here is another scenario, which involves taking out the trash before you ever go to bed that night. Go back to the drive home on day one. You obviously accumulated lots of trash bags of emotions from your day. You load them up just before you drive home. When you notice the drive is less stressful than normal, you begin to reflect on the day and all of the frustrating moments you experienced. You recall being cut off in traffic and how you reacted. Maybe it's never pierced your heart until now how your attitude could have been better in that moment. Was it worth being upset? No. Have you ever cut someone off in traffic before? Probably. So how can you blame them? You identify this is an area you want to work on going forward because it sets a negative tone for the rest of your day. You decide that you really don't want to be that person anymore. It doesn't honor God. So you pray and ask God to forgive you for all the times you weren't being very Christlike in your road-rage moments, and ask Him to help you be more empathic and understanding because it's not worth robbing you of your peace. You feel really good about this decision and feel God's forgiveness as you pray.

You then think about what happened next. You arrived at work late. You were frustrated earlier and really looking for someone or something to blame for being late, but as you reflect, if you are completely honest with yourself, you've noticed you haven't been really responsible with getting up on time, therefore making a habit of running late to work regularly. You wonder why you just can't get up on time, and you blame it on not being able to sleep at night. You decide to set your alarm and no matter how tired you are, you commit to get up because this is a habit you want to break, not someone's fault. You pray and ask the Holy Spirit to get you up in the morning the first time your alarm goes off ready to face the day.

Then you recall how mad you were at your boss when he dropped that project on you that had to be done by noon. You were so mad because you felt like he should have told you yesterday. You start to logically think about what might have been going on with your boss. He honestly may not have known yesterday that this project had to be done today. Or if he did, he could have been putting out so many other fires that it slipped through the cracks, and he just forgot to bring it to you. You ask yourself if you have ever done that before, and honestly have to admit, yes, you have. So you forgive him. You also were frustrated about how he stated you did the task wrong and sent you to change it in a rush. You think about why that bothered you so much. Was it pride because you felt like you knew what you were doing? Was it his tone that made you feel less than in that moment? Or was it because you felt like even doing your best wasn't enough because management failed to train you properly? No matter the reason, it hit your pride, and you were mad. You begin to think about how you should have handled it. What would Jesus have done? You decide you could've handled it more as a team player. If the team needed it done, you were the one chosen to deliver. When you did it wrong and received instruction on how to correct it, you had the opportunity to embrace that moment as a chance to learn. You could be grateful for the knowledge you gained from it.

You assess how you reacted as far as what attitude you gave to the boss amid your frustration. You know you stormed off, so you call your boss to tell him you were frustrated earlier for no good reason. You apologize for not being more of a team player at that moment. Your boss thanks you for calling and says it's all OK. He was shocked at your honesty and appreciated your call. What you don't see is that when you hang up the phone, your boss, in disbelief at your humbleness, begins assessing his own actions thinking, "I should really be better myself! That took courage to own it and apologize." Not only did you clean up your side of things, but you also planted seeds of Christlikeness in your boss's heart and mind.

Now you move on to the waiter at the restaurant. You were pressed for time but didn't lash out or speak up at the restaurant. You just left mad. You don't feel the need to find the waiter tomorrow and apologize, but you talk to God about your lack of patience. You were stressed and frustrated when you went to the restaurant in the first place. The mix-up with your order could have been a random occurrence or a repeated issue you've had at this particular place. If you've experienced this same situation at the restaurant on more than one occasion, you start feeling sorry for whoever is struggling with their job that much that it's a repeated thing, and you begin to pray to God to help them rather than judging them. And while you're at it, you ask God to help you with your attitude toward others at the moment; that you want to be able to give people grace, knowing that we are all just trying to get through each day and do our best.

It's now time to address the final situation you recall which is how you treated your coworker. You know beyond a shadow of a doubt that you were in the wrong and hurt your coworker with your words. You feel really bad about how you acted. You call your coworker to apologize for your behavior, even affirming that they were right with what they said back to you at that moment. You really were being out of line. Your coworker immediately shows you grace and forgives you, understanding it was a tough situation, and acknowledges that you had a lot on you. They showed you grace.

By the time you pull into your driveway, you realize you've done your entire inventory, which made your drive go by really fast. You also got rid of all of the trash on the way home, therefore not having to unload it when you got there. Your heart is free and at peace. You have restored your relationship with yourself, with God, and with those you care about. You actually get to rest tonight, sweet peaceful rest. You go to bed and sleep more soundly than you have in a long time. The alarm clock goes off the next morning, and you jump up to face the day.

Now you decide: is inventory worth the commitment to it or not? This is literally what it's like, and is one of the most valuable steps you can take to transform your way of thinking and your quality of life. The more you do it, the more you grow. The more you grow, the less inventory you have to take. You are breaking habits and old thought patterns you've needed to be free from for a long time!

One of the biggest threats to your space on that subdivision lot we described earlier where your new house sits will be pride itself. It's sly and can sneak into your yard when you least expect it. Sometimes pride comes from feeling so good about where your life is now that you begin to forget what got you there. You can start to feel like you don't need the practices that protect you and your future. To prevent this from happening, it is essential to do daily inventory.

Addressing negative moments on the same day they occur diffuses the situations that flare up inside your heart and mind before it turns to bitterness. Daily cleaning out your mental, physical, emotional, and spiritual space keeps peace high and resentments low or nonexistent.

Whether you journal your inventory or you just spend some quiet time reflecting over your day, the idea of a daily inventory is to resolve any issues as quickly as possible. If you need to apologize for something you said or did, apologize to God and to the person right away. If you are hurt, write about it, pray about it, and find empathy so you can forgive.

If you find it hard to forgive, ask yourself if you've ever acted or done the same thing you are begrudging. Forgiveness requires you to separate what the person did from who the person is. Use the same thought patterns you did in steps 4 to 9 in this building process that helped you forgive those old wounds. Below are some questions to consider about daily inventory.

1. What can you do to implement this step regularly in your day?

2. What do you think would be reasons you wouldn't embrace daily personal inventory?

3. Do you feel that making this a daily practice will be valuable to you? Why or why not?

CHAPTER 11

Step 11

We continue to improve our relationship with God by staying in daily contact with Him through meditation, praise, and prayer; and seeking His will for us and the courage to carry it out.

> In all your ways acknowledge Him, And He will make your paths straight.
> —Proverbs 3:6 (NASB)

> For we are His workmanship, created in Christ Jesus for good works, which God prepared beforehand so that we would walk in them.
>
> —Ephesians 2:10 (NASB)

Make My Will Match Your Will

Some people spend years, even lifetimes, searching for their purpose. They pray relentlessly for God to show them and can even get really depressed or lose the joy of life while waiting for an answer. Finding our purpose is very simple, as the verse above plainly states it.

Every one of us was created to do good works. The path has always been to believe in the Gospel of Jesus Christ to be saved, to be baptized as an outward expression of the salvation we have received, and to do good to others. This is why relational healing with ourselves, with God, and with others is critical to fulfill that purpose. Our purpose can't be fulfilled without including God and others in the picture.

So why do people get so hung up on this issue? I've narrowed it down to a few reasons: comparison, coveting, and pride.

Each day you have the opportunity to fulfill your purpose, yet you may be overlooking these opportunities because it doesn't necessarily come with a label, title, or a platform. Maybe you have witnessed someone else doing something that looks amazing and impactful that you want to do the same, to the point of coveting it. Don't get me wrong. It is great to be inspired by others and to even be drawn to the same area of service as others, but only if God called you to it. God won't cosign what He didn't call you to do.

God gave you gifts to do good works. We've previously studied these in this book. Your gifts are not always going to be the same as someone else's gifts. But if you chase their gifts, you will forfeit the use of your own. Comparing yourself to other people or wanting what other people have will not get you any closer to your purpose. Rather, it will do the opposite, separating you from them, from God, and eventually driving you to isolation. You must be willing to embrace and explore the gifts God gave specifically to you.

Another reason you may overlook the simplicity of your purpose is because it may not be what you were really *wanting* to do. Not everyone has a servant's heart to do good to others. If that's the case, first ask God to search you and see where you personally need work on your heart to genuinely serve others with love. Hopefully, you have been doing that through this journey, but if not, now is the time to start. You have to put first things first, which is to clean up your own heart to make room for your purpose. A verse I read every day to remind me that I need to be willing to do the little things first is this:

> The one who is faithful in a very little thing is also
> faithful in much; and the one who is unrighteous
> in a very little thing is also unrighteous in much.
> (Luke 16:10 NASB)

A steward is someone who looks after what has been entrusted to them. The act of stewarding is managing what has been given to you. You must prove yourself to be a good steward of the little assignments God puts in your path before expecting the bigger assignments.

Have you ever been given a job at work that you didn't want to do, and you didn't do your best on it simply because you begrudged having to do it? Did you think it was beneath you to do that specific task? Guess what, God sees that. What if He gives you something to do for His kingdom? Would you begrudge it if you felt it was beneath you? Would you begrudge it when you get into it and realize it's a lot harder than you ever anticipated? Some people pick a purpose they would like to do based on the results they see that feel good. What they don't see is all of the mentally, physical, emotionally, and spiritually draining labor that went into getting those results. The question then is how willing and faithful will you be.

You are called to be a servant of God by doing good to others wherever He leads. Serving others isn't some big grand beautiful display that necessarily puts us in the limelight. It may grow to that one day, but not before becoming humble enough to do the little things for the very people you can serve in your family, in your friend group, in your community, and most importantly, to strangers.

Something I have learned throughout my own journey is that purpose can be an assignment for a season. Some seasons are shorter and some are longer. To remain in purpose means you have to be willing to change and adapt. You also must remain teachable. Sometimes, where God leads you next may be a place you know nothing about. If you remain teachable and have faith, He will equip you with all you need to do the assignment successfully. And sometimes that requires embracing change and learning new things.

To live out your purpose, you must remain in contact with God. You must be open to being chiseled into more Christlikeness as you grow in purpose. Prayer and Bible reading are essential to maintaining your relationship with God. Reading books, journals, devotionals, listening to podcasts or online sermons, etc., help you to stay in purpose.

Sometimes God may draw your attention to an area where He wants to chisel off the old you so He can create a newness within you for an upcoming assignment. If you find yourself feeling conviction in any area, will you be willing to explore those things with God? Are you willing to grow more like Jesus? He will qualify you for any place He leads you. Trust His process. Stay in contact with Him, growing in His goodness and His grace. Here are some questions to get you started:

1. How well are you currently living out the purpose God gave to us all in Ephesians 2:10. Explain.

2. How willing are you to embrace change? Why or why not?

3. Do you feel like you steward the gifts well that God has given you? Why or why not?

4. When you see someone in need, do you help them? Why or why not? Does your answer change if it's someone you know versus a stranger, someone who looks safe versus someone who may not look or act like you, or someone who may be in situations out of your comfort zone? Explain.

5. Do you believe there is some personal work to be done in your heart's posture in order to fulfill God's purpose for you? Explain.

6. How willing are you to do the little things that God puts in your path each day to fulfill His purpose through you? Explain.

7. Where will you find the courage to follow God's direction each day?

CHAPTER 12

Step 12

Having gained a relationship with God and ourselves, we strive to form healthy relationships with others, allowing God to lead, guide, and direct us in all our affairs.

> Above all, keep fervent in your love for one another, because love covers a multitude of sins.
>
> —1 Peter 4:8 (NASB)

> I am giving you a new commandment, that you love one another; just as I have loved you, that you also love one another.
>
> —John 13:34 (NASB)

Love One Another

Now that the work has begun on your relationships, let's take a moment to apply these principles going forward. The way to tell if a relationship is healthy or unhealthy can be found in the following attributes:

1. It displays fruits of the Holy Spirit—love, joy, peace, patience, kindness, goodness, gentleness, faithfulness, and self-control.

2. Love appears to be based on action rather than desires, emotion, and/or feelings only.

3. It allows you the freedom to be yourself—not weighed down and heavy with a lot of expectations to meet to suit the other person.

4. It's a safe place for either party to be vulnerable with one another.

5. It doesn't create anxiety, but rather helps to diffuse it.

6. It doesn't cause you to question your sanity.

7. It's not one-sided or selfish.

8. It respects one another's boundaries.

9. If a romantic relationship, your paths, values, goals, and beliefs are aligned in order to be equally yoked.

Even after doing all the work on yourself, are you now capable of being a healthy participant in a relationship? Some things to consider about yourself are the following:

1. Do you honor your commitments?

2. Can you identify what is healthy and unhealthy in a situation?

3. Can you patiently wait on God's timing?

4. Are you willing to follow God's will over your own or someone else's?

5. Are you able to say no and stick to it?

6. Are you able to take constructive criticism from a mentor or friend?

7. Are you able to be alone and not feel lonely?

8. Are you dedicated to continue the practices that will help you maintain healthy relationships?

Let's go back to the street scene earlier in this book. Imagine walking out into the street to view your lot and what you have now built there. Keep in mind, the structure you are looking at is actually yourself and the space around you. Share your thoughts about the following statements:

1. As you look at it, recall where you have been in the past and describe it below.

2. Now, looking at all the hard work you've done, describe below how you are living your life today.

3. Lastly, as you admire what you've overcome and now embracing your future, describe below who you want to be. This is your character, meaning, you deny your feelings, motives, and desires when they are in opposition to who you want to be.

These are thoughts to ponder at this stage as you begin to integrate with others on an all-new level. If you will allow God to lead you, He won't lead you wrong. Stay close to Him. Invite Him into all areas of your life. Lean on Him. Work all things out with Him first before involving others so that you are not swayed by others who, even with the best of intentions, can lead you wrong. They don't necessarily have access to the knowledge of God's plans for your life. I encourage you to explore these questions above some more and ask God to reveal anything He wants you to see as you move forward. I pray you all have healthy safe relationships that thrive and push you to be the very best version of yourselves! Amen.

Printed in the United States
by Baker & Taylor Publisher Services